SCOTTISH CLANS

FRONT COVER: *Detail of the battle of Culloden from "An Incident in the Rebellion of 1745" by David Morier. Culloden marks both the most tragically flamboyant gesture of the clans and the end of the clan system.* ABOVE: *Inverary Castle, Argyllshire. Seat of the duke of Argyll, head of the Clan Campbell, it was built in the 18th century.*

LEFT: *Chess king (c. 1200) from one of the Norse sets found at Uig in Lewis. The Norsemen began their raids on Scotland in the 9th century and held the Hebrides until the 13th century and Orkney and Shetland until the 15th century. The main challenge to their possessions in the Isles came from Somerled, founder of the Clan Donald, who won a sea battle in 1156 and gained control of the Sudreys—the islands south of Ardnamurchan Point. With these possessions Somerled regarded himself as an autonomous ruler, a precedent followed by his descendants, the MacDonald Lords of the Isles.*

*

ABOVE: *Iona Abbey and St. Martin's Cross. On this tiny island of Iona off Mull, Columba founded a monastery in A.D. 563. It became a centre of Celtic Christianity and Columba's base. From here he penetrated the furthest reaches of Pictland by way of the Great Glen, and at Loch Ness he encountered a formidable sea creature. This first sighting of the Loch Ness monster was later*

recorded in Adamnan's Life of St. Columba. *In A.D. 574 Columba performed the first Christian coronation in Britain, at Dunadd, capital of Scottish Dalriada. Four hundred years later, Iona was sacked by King Harald Fairhair of Norway, and it was only in the 19th century that serious restoration work began. The Iona Community, which looks after the island today, was founded in the 1930s.*

*

FACING PAGE: *The Aberlemno Cross Slab showing Pictish warriors. The Picts were a Celtic race who, at the coming of the Dalriadic Scots to Alba (land of the Scots) from Dalriada (land of the Irish), controlled the entire east of the country, north of the Forth. They were converted to Christianity by Columba. Later, weakened by persistent Viking raids, they were pacified by Kenneth MacAlpin, king of the Dalriadic Scots, and united with the Scots in A.D. 853. Thereafter they were completely absorbed by the Scots and virtually disappear from history.*

2

SCOTTISH CLANS

Alan Bold

TODAY there is great interest in the Scottish clans but as a social institution the clan system received its death-blow, with the clansmen, at the battle of Culloden in 1746. Clans loyal to the Stuarts were mercilessly punished by order of the Duke of Cumberland, and the English and Scottish Lowland establishments combined to rid the self-styled civilised world of the menace persistently posed by a troublesome race of hillmen. Highland dress was proscribed, the clans were disarmed, and even the bagpipes were banned as an instrument of war.

Visiting the Highlands in 1773 Dr. Samuel Johnson observed the impact of these measures. "The clans", he wrote, "retain little now of their original character, their ferocity of temper is softened, their military ardour is extinguished, their dignity of independence is depressed, their contempt of government subdued, and the reverence for their chiefs abated. Of what they had before the late conquest of their country, there remain only their language and poverty."

So it was no coincidence that when the government lifted the restrictions on Highland dress in 1782 it could stand back to watch the Highland Clearances begin. Resistance was not anticipated and, in the event, not forthcoming. Instead the indigenous population of the Scottish Highlands was removed to make the land fit for sheep to be reared in. As for the chiefs, they were now no more nor less than landlords and sheep were more commercially viable than clansmen. The clan system was eradicated, the clansmen emigrated or went into military service or became crofters, and Britain was finally free of the recalcitrant Celts.

To understand how the clansman was resuscitated to become a national folk-hero and the mainstay of the tourist industry, it is necessary to follow his rise and fall into posthumous grace.

Post-Roman Alba was divided among four groups three of whom—the Picts, the Scots and the Britons—were of Celtic origin. The fourth group, the Angles, who settled in Lothians, were part of that savage fifth-century Teutonic invasion of (what is now) England that scattered the native Britons into Strathclyde, Wales and Cornwall. As far as Alba was concerned the immediate future was to be in the hands of the Picts and Scots.

The Scots came to Alba from Antrim in Northern Ireland to establish a colony in and around Argyllshire. They called their colony Dalriada after their mother country in Antrim and adapted so well to the new environment that they eventually preferred it to the original Dalriada. In c.500 Fergus Mor, son of Erc, set up a new dynasty in Dalriada and established a capital at Dunadd. With this permanent foothold in Alba the ambitious Scots began to take steps to extend their influence. To begin with, Fergus and his brothers divided Dalriada amongst themselves, thus forming the first district clans: Cinel

Continued on page 4

3

Lorn, Cinel Garran, Cinel Comgall and Cinel Angus.

It was an Irish Scot who brought a dynasty and territorial ambition to Alba and another Irish Scot, Columba, who brought Christianity (though St. Ninian had, admittedly, made some inroads). When Columba came to Alba in 563 the Picts controlled most of the country north of the Forth. From his small monastery on the tiny island of Iona, off the west coast of Mull, Columba began to spread Christianity throughout the country. From Dalriada he went up the Great Glen and gradually persuaded the pagan Picts to renounce their Druidic beliefs and embrace Christianity. Columba's great theological victory was the first stage in the Scottish cultural conquest of Pictland.

At the end of the eighth century the Norsemen began to attack the northern coast and islands of Alba. Not only did they permanently transform the character of the Hebrides, the Orkneys and the Shetlands, but the sustained pressure of the Norse raids on the mainland exhausted the Picts. So much so that in 843, when Kenneth MacAlpin the king of the Dalriadic Scots had established a controversial claim to the Pictish throne, he was able to win

*　　　*　　　*

ABOVE LEFT: *St. Margaret's Chapel, Edinburgh Castle. This 11th-century chapel commemorates the Saxon wife of Malcolm Canmore. She was a powerful personality and used her influence to open the gulf between the Saxon and feudal Lowlands and the Celtic and clannish Highlands.*

FACING PAGE: *Although the bagpipes are popularly associated with the clans, the Celtic harp, or Clarsach, was originally the distinctive Highland instrument. The Lamont Harp shown here may be the oldest surviving Clarsach. It was probably brought from Argyll by a daughter of the Lamont family on her marriage to Robertson of Lude in 1464.*

LEFT: *The bagpipes became established in the 16th century when Alasdair Crouchback, 8th chief of MacLeod (1481–1547), founded a College of Piping at Borreraig for the Mac-Crimmons of Skye, hereditary pipers to the MacLeods of Dunvegan. This set of bagpipes was played at Waterloo by George Mackay and by James Mackay at the entry of George IV into Edinburgh.*

4

the argument convincingly. As king of the Scots and kinsman of the Picts he had himself crowned king of both at the Pictish sacred centre of Scone.

This union of the Picts and the Scots under the Dalriadic king meant the end of Pictland and the beginning of the dominance of the Gaelic-speaking Scots. It was not, because of the work of Columba, a sudden event. Yet now the Picts had a religion, a culture and a king imposed on them and in time they were absorbed completely by the Scots. However in swallowing the Picts, the Scots changed their own culture (one example of reciprocal influence being the ability of the Highland bards to memorize genealogies, a technique that derived from the Druids who forbad written records).

In 1018 the Celtic king Malcolm II defeated the Angles at Carham bringing the Lothians under Scottish rule and when, the same year, the king of the Strathclyde Britons died his throne passed to Malcolm II's grandson, Duncan, who in 1034 became king of a geographically united Scotland. The Celts had inherited the earth but were not to control the kingdom. In 1040 Duncan was killed in battle (not, despite Shakespeare, in bed) by Macbeth who was killed in turn by Duncan's son Malcolm in 1058. Malcolm III, or Malcolm Canmore (from the Gaelic *Ceann Mor* meaning "great chief") is credited with alienating the Gaels and initiating that antagonism between clans and crown that is so evident in Scottish history. Full credit, however, should go to his wife.

Because of his English upbringing Malcolm preferred the Anglo-Saxon Lothians to the Celtic north. In 1066 he had himself crowned at Dunfermline rather than Scone. Rather more dramatically, that year saw the Normans conquer England and an influx of Saxon refugees into the Lothians. Malcolm welcomed them with open arms and even married one of them: the Princess Margaret, sister of Edgar the Atheling. She was beautiful, fanatically religious, and a much more powerful personality than her illiterate husband. Under her influence Malcolm substituted Saxon for Gaelic as the court language, tried to force Roman Catholic rituals (like celibacy and poverty) on the Celtic clergy, and introduced feudalism into Celtic Scotland.

In principle, feudalism is the antithesis of the clan system. Under the clan ideal the land was held communally and administered by the chief. Under feudalism all land was royal land. Moreover feudalism superimposed the central crown authority over the authority of the clan chief. It made the king the supreme landowner and subjects vassals. As the clans had evolved from the Dalriadic divisions and the Pictish tribes the loyalty of the clansmen was that of kinsmen to their chief, not subjects to their king. The determination of successive kings to replace clannishness by feudalism drove a wedge between the Celtic Highlands and the Saxon Lowlands that continued up to Culloden.

Given the geography of the Scottish Highlands, it is not surprising that the Scottish kings found it difficult to assert their authority over people who lived among remote and inaccessible mountains. North of the Highland Line (that imaginary frontier stretching diagonally from the Clyde to the Tay) the clans associated themselves with well defined natural areas that they claimed as family property. Deep glens surrounded by mountains and secure mainland areas became inhabited by clans: the Campbells in mid-Argyll, the Camerons in Lochaber, the Robertsons in Rannoch, the MacKays in Sutherland. Islands, too, attracted the great families: the MacDonalds in Islay, the MacLeans in Mull, Tiree and Coll—while Skye was shared by MacDonalds, MacLeods and MacKinnons.

Despite the poverty of the soil, the clans attempted to be self-sufficient units living on the small cattle that somehow managed to survive the mountains. In the islands and on the coast the clansmen caught fish and

Continued on page 6

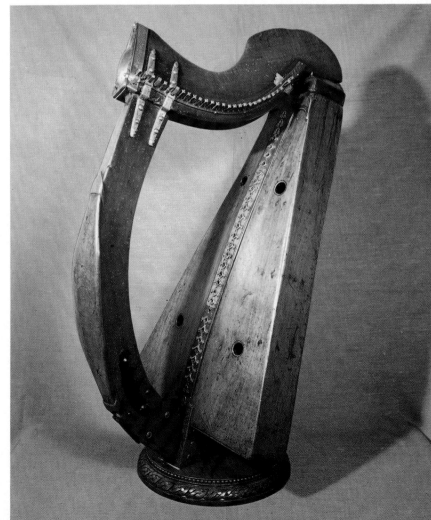

5

exported their surplus to the Lowlands. In the glens they had barley for fermenting whisky (mainly for the edification of the chief and gentlemen) and oats for making bread. It was a harsh way of life for the clansmen and, because cattle had to be protected, these Celtic hillsmen developed endurance and great military skill. In time their impetuosity in battle would startle Lowlander and Englishman alike.

In war and in peace the finest clan quality was solidarity behind the chief. Ideally a clan was one big happy family—literally. *Clann* is the Gaelic word for children and *Mac* is the Gaelic prefix for "son of". So the phrase Clan MacDonald means "Family of the son of Donald". As patriarch, the chief was territorially omnipotent and decided, largely on his own, what was good for the rest of the family. In theory he had to obtain the consent of the rest of the

*   *   *

LEFT: *Cross-shaft from the island of Texa, off Islay, showing Ranald, founder of Clanranald. The Clan Donald, the greatest of the clans, split into several branches of which Clanranald was one of the most important. In the 14th century, in return for resigning the High Chiefship of Clan Donald and Lordship of the Isles to his younger half-brother (at the request of his twice-married father) Ranald gained control of the Outer Hebrides and the mainland around Moidart.*

FACING PAGE, far right: *More effective than the bagpipes in battle was the claymore (from the Gaelic Claidheamh-Mor, meaning "great sword")—a variation of the European two-handed sword. This 16th-century tomb-slab of Murchard Macfie, chief of the Macfie clan, from Oransay island, shows the Highland two-handed claymore. Although horribly effective if on target, a miss could be countered by a more mobile opponent. So, during the 16th century, the basket-hilted broadsword replaced the claymore as the favourite weapon of the clansmen.*

FACING PAGE, right: *Some weapons used by clansmen. Top: the dirk, used with the wooden shield or targe (bottom), which was covered with hide. Centre: Mid 18th-century Highland pistol of steel, with scroll butt. Thus equipped, the Highlander was a formidable fighting machine and when he charged screaming at the enemy, broadsword raised, the effect was terrifying.*

clan before waging war. In practice he made his decision and the others stood by it. When Lochiel, chief of Clan Cameron, pledged his support to Bonnie Prince Charlie he said: "I'll share the fate of my Prince, and so shall every man over whom nature or fortune hath given me any power." By then though, feudalism had made the chief a landlord as well as a patriarch.

In peace, as well as in war, the chief was the supreme law-giver. When he did not personally dispense justice he delegated those who did: a brieve acted as judge and was entitled to a proportion of fines imposed. Although the chief might listen to a council of chieftains for advice on various matters, the clansmen had to accept the authority of the head of the family. Errant children were simply not tolerated. Of course, it worked both ways. The tie of kinship, real or imagined, made for a powerful social unit and the attractions of that were so apparent in the Highlands that individuals and groups applied to the clans for protection. To distinguish them from the *native men* who were connected to the clan by consanguinity, those not protected by the clan were called *broken men*.

In the hierarchy of the clan the chief was followed by the tanist, the commander, the chieftains, the gentlemen and the clansmen. Tanistry, the system of succession by a previously elected member of the family, determined a continuity of strong command (unlike feudal primogeniture). The chief nominated his successor who thereafter bore the title tanist. After the tanist came the commander, military leader of the clan. If the chief was fit enough, he held this position; if old or infirm he appointed a chieftain. Chieftains were the heads of the branches into which the clans were divided. Next to them came the gentlemen, who claimed a blood connexion with the chief. Last, but greatest in numbers, were the clansmen themselves who did the manual work in peacetime and the fighting in wartime.

Although this hierarchy was scrupulously observed there was no feeling of resentment on the part of the clansmen, whose powers of reflection were limited by their circumstances. They were proud to be connected to their chief and to each other and the evidence shows they were willing to die for the clan. To add to the solid-

Continued on page 10

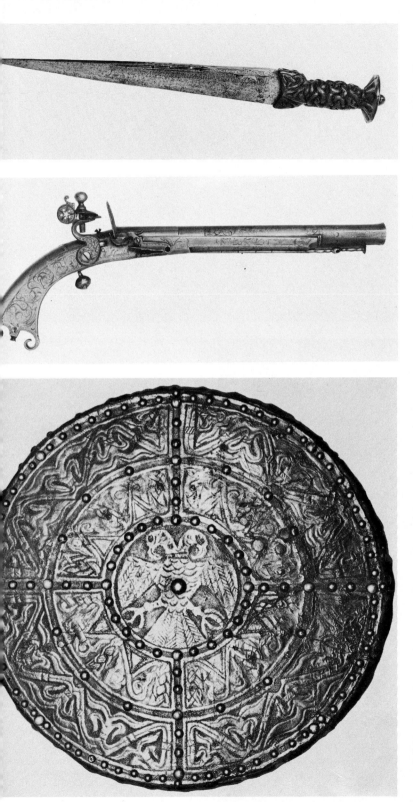

ABOVE: *Ruins of the castle of the Wolf of Badenoch, Loch-an-Eilean, Inverness-shire. Alexander, Earl of Buchan (the wolf of Badenoch), took advantage of the isolation of the Highlands and, though a feudal noble, acted the part of a Highland chief. After being excommunicated for seizing the land of the Bishop of Moray, he led a raid on the Bishop's cathedral at Elgin and sacked it in 1390. This contempt for the central Lowland authority was typical of the Highlanders.*

LEFT: *James VI and I, who united the crowns of two nations, was anxious to see the clans subservient to the crown. Hostility towards the "barbarous" clans manifested itself in several measures designed to convert the Highlanders to Lowland ways. Feudalism was increased, the Statutes of Iona were passed, and a colony of Englishmen and Lowland Scots was set up in Ulster to end alliances between the Celts of Ireland and the Celts of the Isles.*

FACING PAGE, above: *Dunvegan Castle, Skye, the ancestral home of Clan Mac-Leod. In the '45 rebellion several Jacobite clans refused to come out for Charles Edward Stuart because of the lack of French support. The most damaging defections from the Jacobite cause were the MacDonalds of Sleat and the Mac-Leods of Dunvegan.*

FACING PAGE, below: *Duart Castle, Mull. At this 14th-century castle, home of the chiefs of Clan MacLean, nine island chiefs dined before being tricked into boarding a flagship. Later imprisoned in Edinburgh, they were eventually released on condition that they signed the Statutes of Iona (1609).*

arity of the clan the practice of fosterage meant that children (including the chief's) were exchanged and brought up among different families. Thus the most humble clansman felt personally responsible for the children of his chief, and vice versa.

General George Wade, the man whose roads opened up the Highlands, observed something of the clan spirit when he wrote, in his 1724 report to the government on the Highlanders: "Their Notions of Virtue and Vice are very different from the more civilised part of Mankind. They think it a most Sublime Virtue to pay a Servile and Abject Obedience to the Commands of the Chieftains, altho' in opposition to their Sovereign and the Laws of the Kingdom, and to encourage this, their Fidelity, they are treated by their Chiefs with great Familiarity, they partake with them in their Diversions, and shake them by the Hand wherever they meet them." It is typical of this observation that the Highlanders are regarded as being uncivilised.

The first clear personality to emerge in the story of the clans is Somerled, progenitor of Clan Donald, and the main figure in resisting the Norwegians, who controlled the Western Isles as well as Orkney and Shetland. Somerled was an outstanding warrior of mixed Pictish and Norse blood who, after a ferocious sea battle in 1156, gained the Kingship of Man, a Norwegian colony, which put him in control of all the Western Isles from Bute to Ardnamurchan Point. In return for a promise of fidelity David I recognised Somerled's conquests. The difference was this: whereas David thought of Somerled holding his lands directly from the crown, Somerled regarded himself as an autonomous ruler, the King of the Isles.

In 1164, to show his defiance of the crown, Somerled sailed up the Clyde with 150 ships and sacked Glasgow. At Renfrew, however, he encountered the Steward of Scotland's army and was killed. Nevertheless his influence was seminal. Through his politically advantageous marriage to Ragnhildis, daughter of the Norwegian King of the Isles and Man, Somerled left three children, two of whom continued his line: Dougall founded the MacDougalls of Argyll and Lorn; and Reginald (whose son's name was Donald) the MacDonalds of Islay. In his own assertions of independence before the crown Somerled had set a precedent that would be emulated by his MacDonald descendants, the Lords of the Isles.

Not many of the clans acted in concert. Even after the Norse occupation ended in 1266 Scotland was a land where clan fought against clan and the crown despaired of securing their loyalty. For example, although MacDougall of Lorn and MacDonald of Islay opposed Bruce, the Clan Donald followed their chief's brother, Angus Og, and fought on Bruce's right at the battle of Bannockburn. This gesture of allegiance strengthened the position of the MacDonalds and saved the disloyal members of the clan from punitive retaliation by Bruce. (After Bannockburn, the MacDonalds always claimed their place on the right in battle, a tradition disastrously ignored by Lord George Murray at Culloden.)

Divisions within clan groupings were, in fact, the rule rather than the exception as was demonstrated, painfully for those concerned, at the battle of Inverhavon in 1370. The Camerons held land in Lochaber which the Mackintosh claimed was his. Not only did he continually reiterate his claim, but he took cattle from the Camerons as rent. After a particularly vindictive cattle raid, by the Mackintosh, the Camerons rallied 400 clansmen and marched into Badenoch, the territory of Clan Chattan. This confederation of clans included the Mackintoshes, the Davidsons, the Macphersons, the Macgillivrays, the Macbeans and the Farquharsons so, theoretically, it should have been possible for the combined forces of Clan Chattan to defeat the Camerons.

Certainly this was the Mackintosh's

intention when, as Captain of Clan Chattan, he sent the *cran-taraidh* (fiery cross) around Badenoch and gathered the Macphersons and the Davidsons to his cause. Both clans claimed the place of honour on the Mackintosh's right and the argument was still raging when the Camerons arrived to do battle. Forced to make an instant decision, the Mackintosh gave the Davidsons the place on the right and, appalled at this, the Macphersons withdrew from the whole affair. They crossed the Spey and sat down to watch the combat. With a furious charge the Camerons cut the Davidsons to pieces and were in the act of finishing off the Mackintoshes when, at last, the Macphersons consented to join in and soon put the Camerons to flight.

Nor was that the end of the affair. Indignant at the loss of so many clansmen, the Davidsons kept up a campaign of abuse against the Macphersons who countered that, anyway, their clan should have been granted the place on the right. To settle the whole question of priority it was arranged that the argument should be resolved at Perth before King Robert III in 1396. Thirty Macphersons faced thirty Davidsons on the North Inch, a public meadow in Perth, and fought to the death. The Macphersons lost nineteen men and the Davidsons lost twenty-nine men. Nothing was proved. Yet it was undoubtedly to the advantage of the Scottish crown to see the clans

*　　　*　　　*

FACING PAGE: *When the clans were not defying the crown they were mainly concerned with gaining advantage over each other, usually with bloody consequence. During the Civil War, Sir James Lamont received a royal commission to proceed against rebels, including the Campbells, and many atrocities were committed against this powerful neighbour. In 1646 the Campbells retaliated and forced Sir James to surrender his castle on condition that he and his clansmen would be spared. Sir James was imprisoned but the Lamonts were taken to Dunoon churchyard, where 200 were butchered and 36 hanged from a tree. This stone marks the site and was set up by the Clan Lamont Society in 1906.*

RIGHT: *This was the official order for the Massacre of Glencoe signed by Duncanson and sent to Robert Campbell of Glenlyon on 12 February 1692.*

dissipate their energy in feuds against each other, rather than uniting against the central authority. A combination of several clans would be a formidable threat indeed.

Such a threat did materialise under the leadership, inevitably, of the Lord of the Isles. Somerled, founder of the Clan Donald, had been King of the Isles and when Angus Og's son John became chief of Clan Donald in 1354 he assumed the title Lord of the Isles. As Lords of the Isles the MacDonalds were the most powerful clan in Scotland. Their authority was almost total on Scotland's western seaboard where they were monarchs of all they surveyed. John's son, Donald, 2nd Lord of the Isles and chief of Clan Donald, was not content with such power and as a preliminary to extending his influence he signed a treaty of alliance with Henry IV of England. Then,

in 1411, his wife's niece the Countess of Ross renounced her Earldom to enter a convent. Donald immediately claimed the vacant Earldom.

Opposing his claim was the Regent Albany's son, Buchan, who was also an uncle of the Countess of Ross. With the Highlander's contempt for litigation Donald decided to win his case by a show of force and set about gathering his allies. He was supported by his own clan, the MacLeans of Mull, the MacLeods of Skye, the Camerons of Lochaber and the Clan Chattan. This force of several thousand clansmen was, in addition, promised help by Henry IV. Seemingly invulnerable they marched confidently towards Aberdeen which they intended to sack. A small MacKay force unsuccessfully attempted to push them back before Donald brushed them aside and

Continued on page 14

11

The Massacre of Glencoe

When William of Orange *(above left)* came to the throne in 1689 his government were uneasy about the Highland clans and sought ways of enforcing their will there. So they issued a proclamation demanding that all chiefs had to take the oath of allegiance to King William by 1 January 1692. Of all the clans, only two chiefs failed to swear by that date—MacDonnell of Glengarry and MacIan

acDonald of Glencoe. The latter duly
gned on 6 January.

However, on the advice of his Secretary
State, William gave the powerful
engarry another chance but vowed to
ach MacIan and his "sect of thieves"
lesson. The order was given to Robert
ampbell of Glenlyon *(left)* who hap-
ned to be a relative, by marriage, of
d MacIan the chief:

*"You are hereby ordered to fall upon the
Rebells, the McDonalds of Glencoe, and
putt all to the sword under seventy, you
are to have a speciall care that the old
fox and his sones doe upon no account
escape your hands."*

The massacre was carried out with brutal
thoroughness—even a six-year-old child
who begged Campbell for mercy was cut
down. Of 200 Glencoe MacDonalds, less

than 40 were butchered—of the others
their houses were burned and they
themselves left to die in the snow. For
his work, Robert Campbell was promoted
to the rank of Colonel. In mitigation it
should be said that after the battle of
Killiecrankie (1689), the Glencoe Mac-
Donalds sacked the lands of Campbell of
Glenlyon, taking his sheep, cattle and
goats back to Glencoe.

pressed on. Then, at Harlaw, in Aberdeenshire, he was confronted by a well-equipped Lowland army led by Alexander Stewart.

In July 1411 an incredibly bloody battle was fought, appropriately known as "Red Harlaw". Donald's men destroyed more than half of the Lowland army (leaving them with a mere 300 men) but, even with his superior numbers, he could not claim the advantage. It was a humiliating psychological defeat for Donald and he knew, when he retreated, that his semi-autonomous position of strength was no longer tenable. He had to renounce his claim to Ross and agree to become a vassal of the Scottish crown. Thus feudalism continued to set the crown over the clans and erode the Highland way of life. As for the MacDonalds, they were never again to pose such a threat to the crown. In 1493 James IV finally abolished the Lordship of the Isles and the title is now the purely nominal possession of the Prince of Wales.

As the MacDonalds fell, the Clan Campbell rose (they take their name from the Gaelic *Cam-beul* meaning "crooked mouth"). James IV, hammering home legalistic and feudal concepts, confirmed many of the chiefs in their lands by royal parchment deed—"sheepskin grants"—emphasising that the vassal clans held their properties directly from the crown. James also gave Campbell of Argyll a three-year lease to several properties formerly held by the Lord of the Isles. With a strong base established in Argyllshire, the Campbells judiciously gave their support to whoever would give them most in return. They also set about completely dominating the land adjacent to them.

Being territorially acquisitive, the Campbells used any means to extend their influence throughout Argyllshire. The fate of the MacGregors illustrates this point. Because they held their land in Argyllshire and Perthshire on the clan principle, the MacGregors had no documentary evidence of ownership. They could appeal to tradition but not sheepskin grants. With crown confirmation of their own possessions, the Campbells began to turn the feudal screw and demand rents from the MacGregors. Naturally the MacGregor clansmen looked to their own chief and found odious the idea of paying rent to *Mac Chaelein Mor* ("great son of Colin", as the chief of Clan Campbell is always known) or any lesser Campbell.

As more and more MacGregor land was seized the clansmen became broken men and the MacGregor chief became a mere tenant of Campbell of Glenorchy. To exist at all the MacGregors began to make frequent cattle raids on Perth and Stirling. They were in a hopeless position and their impotence was underlined when the 10th MacGregor chief attempted to resist Campbell of Glenorchy's power. He was captured and beheaded on 7 April 1570 at Balloch before an audience of invited guests.

By 1603 the Campbells were determined to finish off the MacGregors. To do so they displayed a cunning cynicism that was to characterise the clan at its worst. The Earl of Argyll, chief of Clan Campbell, encouraged a quarrel between the MacGregors and the Colquhouns of Luss, Dumbartonshire. A quarrel with considerable substance—since a MacGregor raid on Luss territory had accounted for 300 cows, 100 horses, 400 sheep and 400 goats.

A 300-strong MacGregor force (with token MacFarlane and Cameron support) met 700 Colquhouns at Glenfruin on 8 February 1603. An audience of students and others from Dumbarton and Vale of Leven had come to watch. Only the most perverse could have enjoyed the spectacle. By splitting their force the MacGregors attacked from two sides and slaughtered 140 Colquhouns for the loss of two MacGregors. James VI, on the point of departing for England to unite two crowns, was furious at this spectacle of bloodthirsty disunity on his own doorstep. Before leaving Scotland he had the Privy Council pass a law outlawing the MacGregors, abolishing the name MacGregor, and prohibiting more than four members of the clan to meet together at one time.

Any hope the MacGregors may have had of help from other clans soon dissolved. Men such as Lochiel, the Cameron chief, and Clanranald enthusiastically persecuted the outlawed MacGregors. And of course *Mac Chaelein Mor* surpassed himself. Alastair MacGregor, the 11th chief, surrendered to the Earl of Argyll in return for a promise of safe conduct to England where he intended to plead his clan's case. Argyll agreed, took MacGregor to Berwick (thus literally keeping his promise), then brought him back to Edinburgh for execution.

(Despite their experience of being outlawed for a total of 139 years—they had a brief respite after the Restoration —when the clan was reinstated in 1775, 826 clansmen acknowledged themselves as MacGregors, thus demonstrating the remarkable emotional cohesion produced by the clan principle.)

The clans, then, were anything but united. They shared customs and a way of life but were forever each other's worst enemies. The only time a substantial group of clans would combine was in support of the Stuart dynasty (though after the Civil War there was always the massive exception of Clan Campbell). There was, on the part of the Catholic clans at any rate, a feeling that the Stuart monarch was the Chief of Chiefs. And yet the Stuarts were not conspicuously friendly towards the clans. When they took an interest, it was to make the Highlands conform to Lowland norms.

James VI and I, for example, weary of hearing about blood feuds and disputes, commissioned Lord Ochiltree—assisted by Andrew Knox, Bishop of the Isles—to establish the rule of law in the Isles. Chiefs like MacLean of Duart, Donald Gorm of Sleat, Clanranald, MacLeod and MacLean of Ardgour dined at Duart Castle before being invited aboard Lord Ochiltree's flagship to hear Bishop Knox preach. They got more than a sermon. Once the chiefs were aboard the ship sailed for Edinburgh where they were imprisoned and only released when they agreed to support Knox in a policy of reforming the Isles.

Continued on page 17

*   *   *

FACING PAGE, left: *John 2nd duke of Argyll (1678–1743). This Hanoverian Commander-in-Chief in Scotland was head of the Campbell clan. After the battle of Sheriffmuir, Argyll's military competence did much to put down the 1715 rebellion in Scotland. In London, however, he was thought to be too magnanimous with his enemies and George I dismissed him.*

FACING PAGE, right: *James Francis Edward Stuart, the Old Pretender (1688–1766). He made three attempts to regain his Kingdom, the last in 1719, after which he went to Rome and later married Princess Sobieski of Poland; his son—Prince Charles Edward—was born in 1720.*

RIGHT: *John 6th earl of Mar (1675–1732), leader of the Scottish Jacobites in the 1715 rising. Known as "Bobbing John" because of his vacillations, he was Secretary of State for Scotland until dismissed by George I. When he failed to be reinstated, he went to Braemar and raised the Standard for James VIII and III and later became his Commander-in-Chief. Although commanding 12,000 Highlanders, he became intimidated by Argyll's military reputation and after defeat at Sheriffmuir he eventually left for France with the Old Pretender.*

Thus nine chiefs met at Iona in 1609 and signed the Band and Statutes of Icolmkill, the so-called "Statutes of Iona". These measures demanded obedience to the king, ensured Lowland education for the

*   *   *

FACING PAGE: *Loch Nan Uamh. On 25 July 1745, Charles and his seven men of Moidart first landed on the Scottish mainland from this coastal sea-loch between Moidart and Arisaig. Walsh's frigate,* la Doutelle, *had brought Charles from France.*

ABOVE, left: *Glenfinnan. Here at the head of Loch Shiel, Charles raised the Standard of the House of Stuart on 19 August 1745. The column was erected in 1815 by a descendant of a devoted Jacobite.*

ABOVE, right: *Prince Charles Edward, the confident Young Pretender who eventually left Scotland, his ambitions unfulfilled. Later the story of his attempt to secure the throne and his escape from the English troops in the Highlands became a legend.*

sons of the gentry, abolished firearms and handfasting (a system of trial marriage practised by the clansmen) and called for the discouragement of drinking and bards (presumably on the grounds that the two go together). The idea, of course, was to spread "civilisation" among the clans.

Although the Statutes of Iona did introduce a more legalistic approach to disputes, the traditional way of Highland strife did not immediately disappear. Shortly after the Statutes had been ratified, for example, Islay was seized by — successively — Sir James MacDonald, then by the Campbells, then by the MacDonalds, then by the Earl of Argyll with a force from London. And as late as 1688, the year of the Glorious Revolution which saw a Stuart king fall and a constitutional monarchy put in the place of a sovereign's divine right, a clan battle was fought in Scotland. This, the battle of Mulroy, the last clan battle of all, took place between the Mackintoshes and the MacDonalds of Keppoch.

The MacDonalds held lands in Lochaber (Glen Spean and Glen Roy) on the clan principle, but the Mackintosh insisted he had crown permission —sheepskin grants—to hold the land. MacDonald scorned such legalities and, sensing trouble, the Mackintosh got royal permission to attack the MacDonalds of Keppoch with an army of his own clansmen, his allies, and a company of royal troops under Mackenzie of Suddie. To meet this force, several sects of Clan Donald united and annihilated the Mackintoshes at Mulroy. Because of this unexpected MacDonald victory and because of the death of a crown officer, regular soldiers were sent to destroy the Keppoch lands and that branch of Clan Donald.

This last of the clan battles was the first time broadswords were used almost exclusively by both sides. The government reaction to it gave the MacDonalds no alternative but to join Bonnie Dundee for whom they fought superbly at Killiecrankie for the Stuart cause. When Bonnie Dundee died at

Continued on page 18

Killiecrankie, the deposed James foolishly replaced him with a regular officer whose lack of understanding of the Highlanders lost him the respect of such as Cameron of Lochiel and MacDonald of Sleat. Within a few days of his appointment they went home. For his part James lost to William of Orange at the battle of the Boyne and Britain was set to enter a new constitutional and commercially prosperous era in which there was no place for the clans. That, at least, was William III's point of view.

When he had consolidated his crown in battle, William decided that something drastic would have to be done about the Highlanders who had taken the side of the Stuarts. To Sir John Dalrymple, Master of Stair, Under-Secretary of State for Scotland, the best solution was a scheme to tame the Highlanders. In this he was aided by William and abetted by John Campbell, Earl of Breadalbane. Breadalbane was given £12,000 to buy loyalty from the clan chiefs but, whatever happened to the money (and Breadalbane refused to account for it) there was no appreciable increase in respect for William on the part of the clans.

Accordingly, Stair intimated to Campbell of Breadalbane that "the Clan Donnel must be rooted out and Lochiel". On the subject of the money, he added: "God knows whether the £12,000 sterling had been better employed to settle the Highlands or to ravage them: but since we will make them desperate, I think we should root them out before they can get the help they depend on."

It was decided that all the clan chiefs should take the oath of allegiance to William not later than 1 January 1692. Those who refused would be met "by fire and sword and all manner of hostility". The date was obviously chosen with care, for the harsh Highland winter would partly immobilise the clansmen, a point not lost on Stair. "The winter time," he observed, "is the only season in which we are sure the Highlanders cannot escape, and carry their wives, bairns and cattle to the hills. . . . This is the proper time to maul them in the long dark nights."

Not surprisingly the clan chiefs took the oath and by 1 January only the powerful MacDonnell of Glengarry and old MacIan MacDonald of Glencoe had defaulted. MacIan had

tried to make his submission at Fort William on 31 December but, in the absence of a magistrate, was forced to go to Inverary. It was a bad winter and MacIan did not reach Inverary until 2 January. With the sheriff-deputy away, he was unable to take the oath until 6 January. At last William had someone to make an example of, and he wrote to his Highland general: "If MacIan of Glencoe and that tribe can be well separated from the rest, it will be a proper vindication of public justice to extirpate that sect of thieves."

So 120 men from the Earl of Argyll's Regiment of Foot, under the command of Captain Robert Campbell of Glenlyon, went to Glencoe to be billeted in the cottages there. The troops were received with the legendary Highland courtesy and for 15 days they shared friendship, food and drink with the Glencoe MacDonalds. Captain Campbell particularly enjoyed playing cards with old MacIan and his sons. Then on 12 February 1692 the Captain received an order from Major Duncanson authorising the massacre of the MacDonalds of Glencoe. He and his men were to "putt all to the sword under seventy" and the slaughter was to begin at 5 a.m. the following morning.

That evening Captain Campbell played cards with MacIan's sons and said how much he looked forward to dining with the chief the next evening. But as the long dark night of 12 February gave way to the morning of the 13th, the soldiers began their work. MacIan was shot in his bed and his wife had her rings wrenched from her fingers by a soldier's teeth. Then 39 clansmen were attacked in their sleep, bound hand and foot, and murdered in the snow. Their cottages were put on fire as fresh snow began to fall. As the other clansmen realised what was happening they started from their beds and ran towards the caves. Many died in the snow, about half the clan survived. Not only was this a hideous crime, but it was a deliberate mockery of that Highland tradition whereby hospitality was offered even to an enemy.

Highlanders have long memories and even today mention of Glencoe arouses high feeling and bitterness. William of Orange may have demonstrated his power and determination, but, by contrast, he made the Stuarts look more attractive than they in fact were. When the parliaments of Scotland and England united in 1707 the clans resented their new status as minority groups in "North Britain" and their hopes were increasingly pinned on the "king over the water" in France: James Francis Edward, "the Old Pretender".

In 1714 George I came to the throne

* * *

FACING PAGE: *Sent to pacify the Highlands, General Wade built between 1726 and 1737 a network of roads and bridges totalling 260 miles. By opening up the Highlands they gave the Government more control over the troublesome clans. This particular bridge is at Aberfeldy and it was built in 1733.*

RIGHT: *Farquhar Shaw in Black Watch uniform. In 1739 a number of independent companies, which had been raised as a safeguard against cattle-thieving and demands for protection money, were formed into the "Highland Regiment", nicknamed the "Black Watch". In 1743 its soldiers marched to London to embark on overseas service, but some, including Farquhar Shaw, mutinied and were arrested and shot. In battle however they gained a reputation as fearless fighters and their costume proved a source of endless curiosity.*

of Great Britain. He was unattractive, poorly equipped intellectually, and largely ignorant of his adopted kingdom. It seemed to Jacobites the ideal opportunity for the restoration of the Stuarts. However their rebellion was slow to get under way. The Earl of Mar had been dismissed by the Hanoverian king from his position as Secretary of State for Scotland, and he spent months trying to persuade George of his loyalty. Only when George made it clear he had no intention of reinstating Mar did "Bobbing John" (as Mar was known for his vacillation) return to Scotland as leader of the Jacobites. In 1715 he summoned the clan chiefs to a grand hunt at Braemar, raised the Standard for James VIII and III and announced that he, Mar, was Commander-in-Chief, Scotland.

It was a poor appointment because, although Mar had a majority of the Highland chiefs behind him, his military incompetence squandered this potential strength. With around 10,000 clansmen Mar took Perth and then rested on his laurels. In fact he had achieved nothing. At Stirling the Duke of Argyll had only 2,000 men and if Mar had not been intimidated by Argyll's military reputation he could have taken Stirling and pressed on to Edinburgh. As it was Mar did nothing positive. In November he decided to march to Auchterarder but by then Argyll had enlarged his army and was ready to take the Jacobites on. At Sheriffmuir the two sides met.

Continued on page 20

Mar's Highlanders performed magnificently against Argyll's men, but what Mar lacked in tactical expertise Argyll had in abundance. The conflict was indecisive, as the old song all too accurately implies:

There is some say that we wan,
And some say that they wan,
And some say that nan wan at a',
    man,

But one thing I'm sure
That at Sheriffmuir
A battle there was that I saw, man.

After the battle the Jacobite clans grabbed what booty they could and made off home with it. At the prospect of another battle (and therefore more booty) with Argyll the clans rallied again early in 1716. Mar, however, settled for retreat and, tired of their

leader's procrastination, the clans deserted. James Francis Edward had the same idea. A month after landing at Peterhead he had seen enough and left Scotland for France in the company of "Bobbing John". After the collapse of the rebellion the Highlanders were left to take the consequences. Punitive measures really began after another Stuart adventure in 1719 when a planned Scottish diversion fizzled out at the pass of Glenshiel.

It was obvious to the government that as long as the Highlands were impenetrable the clans would have the military advantage in any recrudescence of Jacobitism. To even things up, from their point of view, the government gave General George Wade, Scotland's Commander-in-Chief, the task of opening up the Highlands. Wade planned, with great ingenuity, a network of roads beginning at Perth and snaking throughout the Highlands so that the garrisons at Forts George, Augustus and William were connected with Inverness. Under the auspices of a Disarming Act Wade deprived the clans of many weapons although even he must have known that he collected more obsolete claymores than anything else, and that the clansmen were hanging on to their broadswords. Finally, Wade reorganised the six Highland Independent Companies and required them to police the Highlands.

In 1724 General Wade made a report to the government on the Highlands, and this gives the first accurate indication of the population of the Highlands. Wade estimated that there were around 22,000 men capable of bearing arms—of whom more than half would be likely to support a Stuart rebellion. From these figures we can project a total Highland population of around 150,000 at that time. Therefore what the government feared was not the quantity of the opposition, but the quality of fighting the clansmen were capable of. Most feared of all was the Highland charge. This was a pre-emptive strike that depended on sheer recklessness to terrorise the enemy. Advancing three deep the Highlanders would break into small units led by chieftains. With a targe on their left arm, a dirk in their left fist, they rushed forward firing pistols—if they had any—then drew their broadswords and slashed into the enemy. This technique was to become feared during the '45

Uprising. It was to be, in fact, Bonnie Prince Charlie's secret weapon.

Thirty years after his father's failure in the '15 Charles Edward Louis Philip Casimir Stuart landed at Eriskay—a tiny Hebridean island—with seven followers and no armed support. He had come to a country he knew nothing of to take a crown he had never seen. As Scott put it in *Waverley* Bonnie Prince Charlie "threw himself upon the mercy of his countrymen, rather like a hero of romance than a calculating politician". When MacDonald of Boisdale told him to go home Charles said "I am come home". He then predicted that "my faithful Highlanders will stand by me". It was audacious in the extreme yet this approach took him nearer the crown than his father had ever been.

With naive confidence in the justice of his cause Charles won the astute Cameron of Lochiel to his side and on 19 August 1745 raised his Standard at Glenfinnan before some 1,200 clansmen. From Glenfinnan he went from strength to strength, first taking Edinburgh and then spectacularly defeating Sir John Cope at Prestonpans. Bonnie Prince Charlie was in command of all Scotland. That was not, however, enough for a Stuart.

With his 5,000-strong Highland army he marched into England taking Carlisle, Preston, Lancaster, Manchester, Macclesfield and then Derby.

*   *   *

Suddenly, when within 150 miles of London, the Prince's advisers began to panic realising they faced an army some six times larger than their own. The Prince wanted to go on. He had known only victory so far and reasoned that he had an excellent chance of success. Caution, however, prevailed. Although he said: "Rather than go back, I would wish to be twenty feet under ground" Charles was persuaded to retreat. And retreat the Highland army did, as far as Inverness. At Culloden, on 16 April 1746, an exhausted, starving, ill-equipped Highland army were attacked by 9,000 regular troops under the command of the Duke of Cumberland who had never won a battle before.

It took Cumberland only 25 minutes on Culloden Moor to destroy the Highland army. In the circumstances he could hardly have failed. On the day before the battle the Highlanders had eaten one biscuit apiece. On the night before the battle they had taken part in a totally disorganised night march. They were, in short, in no condition to do battle. Cumberland, the "Butcher", showed no mercy. The wounded were left to die, the captured were burned alive and mutilated, the dead were left to rot. After the battle Cumberland destroyed villages and towns he felt were sympathetic to Jacobitism. The Prince escaped, became a fugitive in the Hebrides, then returned to Europe to embark on a pathetic life of debauchery. The Highlanders were crushed: it was only left to break their spirit.

This was done with a new Disarming Act, with a ban on Highland dress, and with a planned campaign to discourage the Gaelic tongue and make the clansmen God-fearing Protestant folk. So successful was this
Continued on page 22

campaign that by 1782 the government could lift the ban on Highland dress. Even the kilt could not revive the broken spirit of the clansmen. They were docile, like sheep. And they were to be replaced by sheep, mainly the Great Cheviot and Blackface breeds. The fighting spirit of the clansmen had gone and they were evicted from the glens and forced to emigrate. The alternative was to join the army and it is significant that between 1740 and 1815 eighty-six Highland regiments were formed.

The clan chiefs, too, played a part in this destruction. With the clan system in ruins they were regarded as mere landlords and it seemed to them that sheep were more profitable than men. On only one occasion did the clansmen protest against this persecution. In 1792 some 400 men from Ross and Sutherland marched south, forcing the Lowland shepherds to herd flocks of sheep before them. Starting from Lairg they got to Alness, 30 miles further south, with

some 6,000 sheep. Then word came that the Black Watch were on the march from Fort George. The Highlanders fled ignominiously and in Gaelic verse this incident was remembered as *Bliadhna nan Caorach,* the "Year of the Sheep".

It may seem strange that Lowland Scotland could rejoice over the extermination of the Highland way of life, but it did. Scotland was *two* nations—one commercially minded in motivation and English in sympathy, the other agricultural and Gaelic in temperament. And yet no sooner was the English-speaking world rid of the clans than it wanted to preserve their memory. It wanted the picturesque costumes without the Gaelic-speaking barbarian inside them. More than anyone else, Sir Walter Scott romanticised the clans and once the movement had begun it became a craze. For example, in 1800 the firm of William Wilson & Son of Bannockburn manufactured very few tartans. By the time of George IV's

visit to Edinburgh they manufactured 150. Today there are hundreds of tartans, with commercial variations being added to them all the time.

George IV's visit in 1822 was the apotheosis of the Highland craze initiated by Scott. Indeed Scott was involved in the arrangements and personally stage-managed the visit. George appeared in kilt and plaid in, naturally, the Stuart tartan. After a dinner in Parliament House George proposed a toast—"Health to the chieftains and clans, and God Almighty bless the Land of Cakes. Drink this with three times three, gentlemen." He also flattered Lady Anne Grant by telling her she was "truly an object fit to raise the chivalry of a clan".

It was only left to Victoria and Albert to make a museum out of their Scotophilia. After holidaying with Victoria at Balmoral, Prince Albert bought the estate, demolished the old castle, and commissioned a grandiose new castle which he personally supervised—right down to the tartan carpets. Victoria called Balmoral her "dear paradise" and could never exhaust its charms or the historical associations of the Highlands. After visiting the Glenfinnan monument in 1873 she wrote in her diary: "What a scene it must have been in 1745! And here was *I*, the descendent of the Stuarts and of the very king whom Prince Charles sought to overthrow, sitting and walking about quite privately and peaceably".

It was true. The clans had been tamed out of existence and only survived in the memory. Yet it is a powerful memory that makes everyone with Scottish connexions long to be affiliated to a clan. A powerful memory that makes the clansmen such an object of adoration all over the English-speaking world. Today there are almost a thousand pipe bands in Scotland, the Scots Ancestry Research Council handles more than a thousand genealogical enquiries a year for Americans alone, there are more than a thousand tartans (though most of them would have baffled the clansmen). Clan societies preserve old castles, international clan gatherings are held, and all the time the motor-car noses its way into the straths and glens looking for evidence that the clans really were what we believe they were.

Now the clans only exist in the dimension of history. At the time of

*   *   *

their defeat they were an anachronism in terms of Lowland economic and social organisation. But they had a language and a culture and a landscape of their own. And they were taken from them. Perhaps the reason that people feel so sentimental towards the clans is that their exit from history was so dramatically total, so tragically sudden. It is a mood perhaps best

expressed in that exile's lament, "The Canadian Boat Song":

From the lone shieling and the distant island
Mountains divide us and a waste of seas;
But still the blood is strong, the heart is Highland
And we in dreams behold the Hebrides.

FACING PAGE: *Balmoral, Aberdeenshire. Prince Albert bought the 24,000 acre estate of Balmoral in 1852 for £31,500. He had already spent holidays there with Victoria in what the queen called "the pretty little castle in the old Scottish style". Albert soon demolished the old castle and commissioned a new one, which he personally supervised down to the tartan curtains and tartan carpets. This grandoise Victorian construction, lavishly decorated, became a "dear paradise" to Victoria. It gave its name to Balmoralism, that irrational worship of all things Scottish.*

RIGHT: *George IV in Highland dress on his visit to Scotland in 1822 by Wilkie. This was the first visit to Scotland by a reigning monarch since Charles II and it put the seal of approval on Scott's campaign to give Scotland a national identity, however idealised.*

The Main Highland Clans

Buchanan
Cameron (MacGrillonie, MacMartin)
Campbell (MacArthur, MacPhun)
Clan Chattan
Chisholm
Colquhoun
Cumming
Clan Donald
Drummond
Erskine
Farquharson
Fergusson
Forbes
Fraser
Galbraith
Gordon
Graham
Grant
Gunn
Hamilton
Hay
Innes
Lamont
Lindsay
Livingstone (Macleay)
MacAlister
MacAulay
MacCallum
MacDonnell
MacDougal
Clan Macduff
MacEwen
Macfarlane
Macfie
Macgregor
Mackay
Mackenzie (Matheson, Macrae)
Mackinnon
Mackintosh (Farquharson, Shaw)
Maclachlan
Maclaren
Maclean
Macleod
Macmillan
Macnab (Dewar)
MacNachtan
Macneil
Macpherson
Macquarie
Macqueen
McCorquodale
Menzies
Moncreiffe
Morrison
Munro
Murray (Moray, Butter, Atholl Highlanders)
Ogilvy
Oliphant
Clan Ranald
Rattray
Robertson (Duncan, Reid)
Ross
Scrymgeour
Sinclair
Stewart
Sutherland
Urquhart
Wallace

ABOVE: *Highland Games at Portree in the Isle of Skye. The modern image of the Highlander : tossing the caber. These games recall traditional clan meetings and are an example of the deep affection Scotsmen feel for that part of their history that was extinguished.*

BACK COVER: *The inscription on the Culloden Memorial Cairn (erected by Duncan Forbes, 10th laird of Culloden, in 1881). The cairn marks the most fiercely contested part of the battlefield; a service is held here annually.*

ACKNOWLEDGMENTS

With the exception of the following all the photographs are reproduced by permission of the Scottish National Portrait Gallery; pp i cover, 17 (right), 22, 23, the Royal Collection by gracious permission of Her Majesty The Queen; pp 1, 3, 4 (top), J. Pugh, A.R.P.S.; pp 2 (bottom), 18, Edwin Smith; pp 4 (bottom), 5, 6, 7, National Museum of Antiquities of Scotland; pp 8 (top), 9 (top), Pix Photos; p 8 (bottom), National Maritime Museum Greenwich; pp 9 (bottom), 13, Noel Habgood, F.R.P.S.; p 11, National Library of Scotland; pp 12 (top), 21, National Portrait Gallery, London; p 17 (left), Laird Parker of Oban; p 19, Scottish United Services Museum; pp 2 (top), 24, British Tourist Authority.

SBN 85372 171 8